DINOSAUR

FACE-OFF!

Scholastic Inc.

How to face-off!

This book features 20 pairs of the most amazing dinosaurs and other monster reptiles. Some pairs might have actually met in a life-and-death battle. Others just lived at the same time. We've given each dinosaur a battle scorecard.

Check out each dino's battle scores. Which skill will it use in the fight? Who wins? You decide!

Contents

T. rex and Triceratops face off on pages 12–13. Their battle scores might surprise you. Armored herbivores had more fight than you might think!

The picture on page 1 is a *T. rex* skull. Its teeth could be six inches long!

ISBN 978-1-338-79464-9
10 9 8 7 6 5 4 3 2   22 23 24 25 26
Printed in China 173
First edition 2022

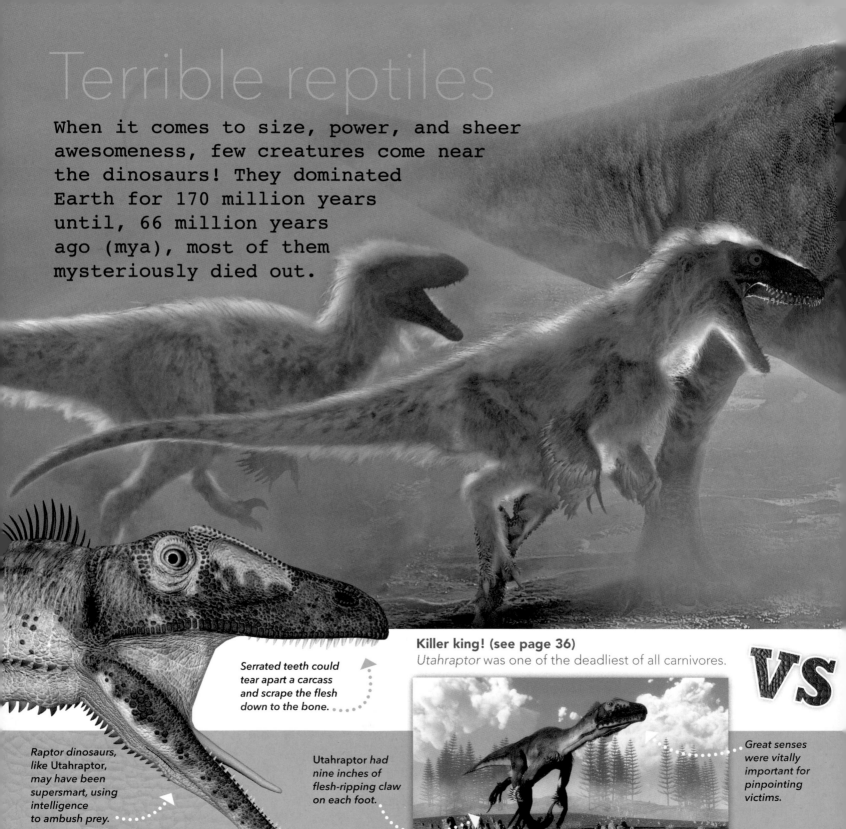

Terrible reptiles

When it comes to size, power, and sheer awesomeness, few creatures come near the dinosaurs! They dominated Earth for 170 million years until, 66 million years ago (mya), most of them mysteriously died out.

Serrated teeth could tear apart a carcass and scrape the flesh down to the bone.

Raptor dinosaurs, like Utahraptor, may have been supersmart, using intelligence to ambush prey.

Killer king! (see page 36)
Utahraptor was one of the deadliest of all carnivores.

Utahraptor *had* nine inches of flesh-ripping claw on each foot.

Great senses were vitally important for pinpointing victims.

VS

Eat or be eaten

The dinosaurs' world was peaceful. Dinosaur battles only broke the spell occasionally. But there was always a struggle for survival. In this book, we introduce the most awesome of these ancient warriors and their prey. Each year, scientists are making exciting discoveries about predator-prey relationships to shine a spotlight on their struggles.

Did the dinosaurs really vanish?

No, they're all around us now! Only, we call them birds. Birds are actually dinosaurs, too. But all the rest, what scientists call "non-avian dinosaurs," did die out 66 mya. And it's those that this book is about.

Defending heavyweight (see page 49)

Kentrosaurus was one of the best-defended herbivores.

Kentrosaurus's intimidating armory of spikes and plates deterred the fiercest carnivore.

Dino weapons

Let's take a look at the weapons the predator dinosaurs had at their disposal. Of course, sometimes predators got lucky and found a fresh corpse. But most of the time they needed to find a kill—and they were armed to the teeth for murder!

Claws
All dinosaur predators had some kind of claw. Some were used for gripping; others for slashing, stabbing, or even climbing. They were made of keratin like your skin, nails, and hair!

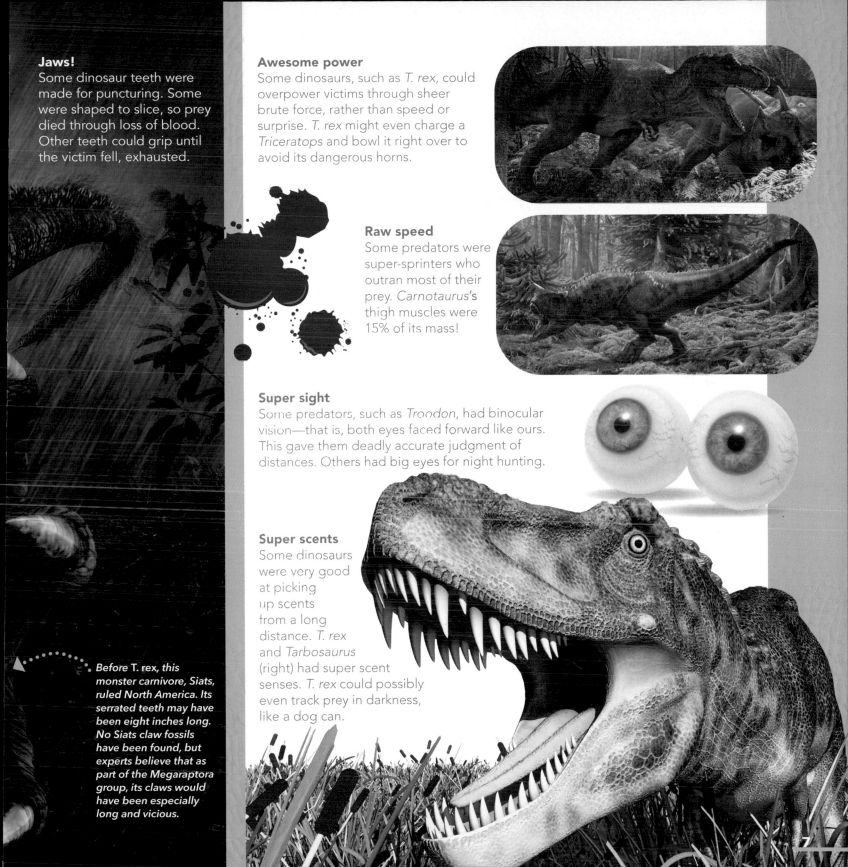

Jaws!

Some dinosaur teeth were made for puncturing. Some were shaped to slice, so prey died through loss of blood. Other teeth could grip until the victim fell, exhausted.

Awesome power

Some dinosaurs, such as *T. rex*, could overpower victims through sheer brute force, rather than speed or surprise. *T. rex* might even charge a *Triceratops* and bowl it right over to avoid its dangerous horns.

Raw speed

Some predators were super-sprinters who outran most of their prey. *Carnotaurus*'s thigh muscles were 15% of its mass!

Super sight

Some predators, such as *Troodon*, had binocular vision—that is, both eyes faced forward like ours. This gave them deadly accurate judgment of distances. Others had big eyes for night hunting.

Super scents

Some dinosaurs were very good at picking up scents from a long distance. *T. rex* and *Tarbosaurus* (right) had super scent senses. *T. rex* could possibly even track prey in darkness, like a dog can.

Before T. rex, this monster carnivore, Siats, ruled North America. Its serrated teeth may have been eight inches long. No Siats claw fossils have been found, but experts believe that as part of the Megaraptora group, its claws would have been especially long and vicious.

Dino defenses

Now let's look at the range of defenses the plant-eaters could use. They faced some of the most terrifying killers that ever stalked the Earth, such as *T. rex* and *Utahraptor*. But they weren't ready to roll over and be lunch.

FRILL BRILL Some dinosaurs, like *Styracosaurus*, had a huge frill of bone around their necks. This may have been a fashion statement just for show, but it probably helped protect their vulnerable necks, too.

HEAD BUTT Lots of plant-eating dinosaurs had seemingly outsize, bony heads. Why? They could use them like a battering ram to drive off opponents.

ALARM CALL Some dinos had bony crests they could sound like a great trumpet and send the alarm out about an attack.

CAMOUFLAGE Little evidence about dinosaurs' color survives. But chances are they used camouflage like modern animals. Armored *Borealopelta* was mottled reddish-brown. This confuses the eye like a zebra's stripes.

SIZE Some plant-eaters were too big for even the fiercest predator. *Mapusaurus* was as big and vicious as *T. rex*, but it was dwarfed by gentle giant *Argentinosaurus*. But even supersized dinosaurs started as babies. So the message is, grow up! Fast!

ARMOR Bony armor could deter a predator. *Ankylosaurus* was the tank of the dinosaur world, covered with tough, bony plates and spikes. Even *T. rex* needed a can opener!

FLAIL TAIL Some dinosaurs, like *Ankylosaurus*, had a tail with a heavy lump of bone at the end. They could use it to smash an attacker's legs like a sledgehammer.

SPIKES Sharp spikes were used to attack and made a dino tricky to eat! *Bajadasaurus* had spikes pointing forward. *Sauropelta* had major spikes to protect its neck and shoulders.

TAIL WHIP Sauropods might look like an easy touch with no weapons—but you wouldn't want to get in the way of their heavy tails, which they could whip fast enough for a sonic boom!

TAIL SPIKES *Stegosaurus* was a spiked dinosaur with an extra weapon in its armory—giant spikes on its tail, which it could whip around to skewer an attacker.

SPEED For smaller dinosaurs, by far the best escape was to run away fast and hide. *Deltadromeus* ("delta runner"), which lived where the Nile Delta is now, was built like a smaller, slimmer *T. rex*.

HORNS With sharp horns, dinosaurs could charge any attacker, or lunge upward to rip into its belly. Some dinosaurs had a single horn, and some had three or even five! *Triceratops*, *Torosaurus*, and *Coahuilaceratops* all had horns over 4 feet long.

Dino diversity

The variety of ancient dinosaur life was incredible. More than 1,000 species have been named, though some might simply be young versions of adults. Figuring out how they relate is tricky, since experts often have just small fragments to go on.

Like a dino?
Dinosaurs were reptiles, like lizards or crocodiles, but they were more like birds and mammals than you might think! Most experts now believe that birds are directly descended from dinosaurs. Unlike modern reptiles, many dinosaurs were covered in feathers or down. They were possibly warm-blooded. And many were bipedal, able to move on two legs, like modern birds and humans do.

This feathered dinosaur, *Microraptor*, may have been able to fly.

Hipsters
Experts divide dinosaurs up according to the shapes of their hips. Dinosaurs with hips like birds are called the Ornithischia. Those with hips like lizards are called the Saurischia. Lizard-hipped dinos are divided up again by the shape of their feet, into sauropods (lizard foot) and theropods (beast foot).

Theropods
The predators of the dino world, theropods were mainly terrifying meat-eaters—like *T. rex* and *Utahraptor*. They walked mostly upright on two strong legs, and had three-toed, birdlike feet, with sharp claws and short arms. Most had a killer bite.

Argentinosaurus's sheer bulk would have intimidated any theropod.

This theropod, Mapusaurus, targeted weak or young Argentinosaurus.

Bird-hipped
The bird-hipped dinos were all placid herbivores, but many had serious armor, like *Triceratops*.

Sauropods

The earthshaking gentle giants of the dinosaur world fed only on plants. Sauropods walked on all four feet, had massive bodies and small heads, and long necks and tails.

Triceratops's armored head was one-third of its total size.

Changing planet

Dinosaurs survived through three entire geological periods, the Triassic (250–200 mya), Jurassic (200–145 mya), and Cretaceous (145–66 mya) periods. They had to adapt to ever-changing habitats and even shifting continents. For 100 million years, the world's land was one supercontinent, Pangea. At the start of the Jurassic period, Pangea began to split up.

200 mya
Early Jurassic. Pangea splits into two, with Laurasia in the north and Gondwana in the south.

150 mya
Late Jurassic. The continents are arranged in a giant horseshoe around the Tethys Sea.

100 mya
Cretaceous. Today's continents are separate island landmasses.

50 mya
Paleogene. The age of dinosaurs is long gone and the continents are moving toward today's position.

Coelophysis

Triassic desert

The world was superhot in Triassic times, good for reptiles. Early dinos, like *Coelophysis*, appeared to make the most of the fringes of scorching deserts.

Jurassic swamp

In Jurassic times, the world cooled, continents shifted, and flooded areas became swamps, lush with plants. Herbivores grew massive on the plants; predators grew massive on the herbivores. Vast reptiles began to claim the skies.

Jurassic ocean

The movement of the continents also created shallow, warm oceans teeming with life. Reptile predators, such as pliosaurs and plesiosaurs, grew to gigantic sizes on all the food, out-sizing many dinosaurs.

Cretaceous plains

In Cretaceous times, the world heated up again, and the land was drier. The most famous dinosaurs of all time, like *T. rex*, lived on the plains, in the forests, and on the riverbanks. Dinosaurs broke all-time size records.

TYRANNOSAURUS REX

Vents on the head helped T. rex stay cool while crushing prey.

T. rex was probably scaly, with feathers on its back. Its arms couldn't reach its mouth!

Tyrannosaurus rex was an absolute monster. One of the most awesome predators that ever stalked the earth. Almost forty feet of sheer killing power! It might have had small front paws, and you could outrun it on a bicycle. But that bite! Aaargh! It could crunch right through a car, passengers and all.

Mega bite

The saltwater crocodile has the most powerful bite of any animal alive today at a frightening 3,700 pounds. But *T. rex* had a bite well over twice as powerful at 8,000 pounds—all focused on its mega-sharp teeth. Perfect for crunching bones of other big dinosaurs!

Bone crunching

We know *T. rex* could bite through big dinosaurs because scientists have found bones in its poop. And yes, it had chunks of bones from the huge *Edmontosaurus*.

- **NAME:** Tyrant lizard
- **TIME:** 67–66 mya
- **HABITAT:** Warm, swampy forests
- **DIET:** Maybe, large dinosaurs
- **LOCATION:** Western North America

VS TRICERATOPS

Triceratops was number one on *T. rex*'s menu, but this mild-mannered plant-eater was no pushover. Even though it was superheavy, it was no slouch when running. And even *T. rex* with its mega bite would think twice before facing *Triceratops*'s armored head with its three skin-busting horns and no-nonsense frill.

- **NAME:** Three-horned face
- **TIME:** 67–65 mya
- **HABITAT:** Forests and scrub
- **DIET:** Plants
- **LOCATION:** Western North America

The two main horns could be up to four feet long and incredibly sharp.

Great defender
One fossil from Montana has a largely complete *Triceratops* near a *T. rex*. *T. rex*'s teeth were found by *Triceratops*'s fossils, but *T. rex*'s skull was cracked. Experts are trying to figure out what went down.

Dino display
Triceratops had a giant frill of bone, studded with spikes. It might have helped protect its neck from dangerous bites. But it was more likely for showing off and attracting a mate.

Triceratops had a beaklike mouth and powerful jaws with rows of sharp teeth for shredding tough plants.

CARNOTAURUS VS

Carnotaurus may have been smaller than *T. rex* and its mouth was less powerful, but whoa, was it probably fast! Powered by a muscular tail, it could outsprint the fastest racehorse! Its only problem was turning. So it just crashed straight through things. The only way to escape it was to keep changing course.

Open wide

Carnotaurus did not have a big head and super-strong jaws. But, like snakes and crocodiles, it could open its mouth very wide. *Carnotaurus* got its name, meaning meat-eating bull, from the stubby, bull-like horns over its eyes. They may have been used for contests with other *Carnotaurus*.

NAME: Meat-eating bull
TIME: 70 mya
HABITAT: Possibly around lakes
DIET: Medium and small dinosaurs
LOCATION: Argentina

Long, slender legs, perfect for running, are a big contrast to little arms and hands!

See in 3D

Carnotaurus had small eyes and poor eyesight, but both eyes faced forward, giving it some "binocular" vision—the 3D view of the world that humans have. *Carnotaurus* probably hunted mainly by its keen sense of smell.

This is my patch

Pairs of *Carnotaurus* may have claimed a patch of good hunting territory and defended against rivals, just like modern hawks do in woodlands. They'd raise their young there, away from others of their kind, who might like their babies for lunch!

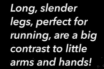

DO NOT ENTER

ANKYLOSAURUS

BATTLE SCORE

Ankylosaurus was probably the best-armored creature that ever lived, with a mighty club on its tail.

ATTACK SCORE: **5/10**
DEFENSE SCORE: **10/10**
SPEED: **6 mph**
LENGTH: **28 ft**

If you walked fast, you could easily overtake *Ankylosaurus*. But it was built like an absolute tank! *Ankylosaurus* was encased in teeth-breaking, super-thick armor made of massive knobs and oval plates of bone, known as osteoderms. It even had an armored faceplate!

As if the armor wasn't enough, Ankylosaurus had two rows of spikes along its back.

Swing that club

Ankylosaurus could put up a fight, too. Its club tail contained fused vertebrae. A big swing, and it could destroy an attacker's legs.

Ankylosaurus not only had armor but a broad, flat body, which made it hard for an attacker to get a grip.

NAME: Fused lizard
TIME: 70–65 mya
HABITAT: Coastal plains
DIET: Plants
LOCATION: North America

R.I.P.

How to kill an *Ankylosaurus*

Ankylosaurus's armor was so tough that it could just sit there and take just about anything. But there was little armor on its belly, so the best way to kill an *Ankylosaurus* was to flip it over. Easier said than done, though. It was very wide and low-slung—and superheavy.

MAJUNGASAURUS

Majungasaurus was related to *Carnotaurus*, but it was only just fast enough to catch slowly lolloping sauropods, and its stubby snout was perfect for latching onto its prey with its teeth until the prey was exhausted. Tooth prints in *Majungasaurus* fossils reveal a big secret.

Dinner's on me
Scientists have found tooth prints in *Majungasaurus* fossils similar to those in their prey. They've concluded that these dinos, in desperate times, were cannibals!

The hands of Majungasaurus *were tiny and stiff. So it was its mouth that did the work.*

- **NAME:** Mahajanga lizard
- **TIME:** 72–66 mya
- **HABITAT:** Beside coasts and rivers
- **DIET:** Sauropod dinosaurs
- **LOCATION:** Madagascar

Show horn
Majungasaurus had a crest-like horn on its head. But the bones beneath were too weak for serious fighting. So it was probably mainly for show.

I am not a vegetarian
When the first *Majungasaurus* remains were discovered in Madagascar in 1896, researchers thought it was a kind of Pachycephalosaur, as it had a knobbly head. It was only recently confirmed to be a carnivore.

VS PACHYCEPHALOSAURUS

Pachycephalosaurus had just about the thickest skull you can imagine. It had a domed cap of bone almost ten inches thick—so thick scientists once thought it was a kneecap, except dinosaurs don't have kneecaps. Maybe it was a kind of crash helmet.

BATTLE SCORE

Pachycephalosaurus had a spiky crash helmet of bone, but that was really only a defense against other *Pachycephalosaurus*!

ATTACK SCORE: **2/10**
DEFENSE SCORE: **5/10**
SPEED: **Unknown, maybe 15 mph**
LENGTH: **14.5 ft**

Head bangers
No one knows why these dinosaurs had such thick skulls. It may have been to protect against *T. rex* bites, or for head- or flank-butting rivals.

Inside the horny beak were two sets of teeth for ripping off and chewing leaves, and maybe fruits and nuts.

Show-off
As well as its domelike skull, *Pachycephalosaurus* had spiky crowns on its nose and behind its head—maybe for defense, or maybe just for show.

Pachycephalosaurus ran on two big, strong legs, and had only short arms.

- **NAME:** Thick-headed lizard
- **TIME:** 75–65 mya
- **HABITAT:** Coastal plains
- **DIET:** Plants
- **LOCATION:** North America, Madagascar, Mongolia, Southern England

Wizard dino
In 2006, a new *Pachycephalosaurus* species was named *Dracorex hogwartsia*, the "dragon king of Hogwarts," after the fictional Hogwarts School of Witchcraft and Wizardry in the Harry Potter books by J.K. Rowling.

EDMONTOSAURUS

Edmontosaurus is one of the best known of all American dinosaurs. That's partly because there were lots of them, living in big herds. But maybe also because it had super tough skin, which has often survived along with the bones. The mummified skin shows they may have had striped camouflage, like zebras.

Surviving skin shows this dinosaur was covered in small, non-overlapping scales.

Beak and teeth
Edmontosaurus could chew just about anything, including pine needles. It had a sharp beak and a thousand teeth. Yes, a thousand! It was probably the best chewing machine ever.

NAME: Edmonton lizard
TIME: 73–66 mya
HABITAT: Beside coasts and rivers
DIET: Conifer needles and horsetail ferns
LOCATION: Western North America

Even *T. rex wouldn't want to get in the way of a charging herd* of Edmontosaurus, *each weighing over four tons and moving as fast as a bus.*

Monster family
Edmontosaurus were some of the largest dinosaurs living toward the end of the dinosaur age. Yet they were very social animals, nesting together and gathering in herds for mutual support, rather like oxen and wildebeests today. An *Edmontosaurus* herd on the move must have been an awesome sight.

VS EUOPLOCEPHALUS

Euoplocephalus, like its cousin *Ankylosaurus*, was absolutely covered in a supertough armor of bone. Even its eyelids were armored. If a *T. rex* came hunting, it was too lumbering to run, but it could hunker down and wait it out. It might even give a bone-breaking swing of its club tail.

BATTLE SCORE

Euoplocephalus was one of the best-armored beasts ever, slow-moving but built like a tank.

ATTACK SCORE: **2/10**
DEFENSE SCORE: **8/10**
SPEED: **6 mph**
LENGTH: **20 ft**

Bumper car

Euoplocephalus had poor eyesight, so thank goodness for its tough armor. Weighing two tons, *Euoplocephalus* was twice as heavy as an Indian rhino of today.

Euoplocephalus might have had a mighty tough head, but it had a really tiny brain for its size. Only sauropods had smaller brains for their size!

It ate and digested a huge amount of low-lying plant material, so it must have had a big gut and let out monster farts!

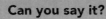

NAME: Well-armored head
TIME: 70 mya
HABITAT: Coastal plains
DIET: Plants
LOCATION: North America

Can you say it?

Even scientists have trouble with this dino's name! Try saying You-oplo-SEFF-a-luss! The "eu" part comes from the ancient Greek word for "well," the "oplo" is ancient Greek for "armored," and "cephalus" the ancient Greek word for "head." Not a name to mess around with!

TROODON

Some people say *Troodon* was the smartest dinosaur of all. It was quite small, but for its size, its brain was several times bigger than most other dinosaurs'. It also had binocular, 3D vision. It was nimble, and its sharp brain helped it survive in more extreme, colder climates.

Tooth first

Troodon's name means "wounding tooth." A tooth was all that was found of it at first, in 1856. More remains were only discovered in the 1930s. Even now, experts aren't quite sure about it, and the word Troodontidae covers a mixed bag of creatures.

- **NAME:** Wounding tooth
- **TIME:** 74–66 mya
- **HABITAT:** Forests
- **DIET:** Probably omnivore
- **LOCATION:** North America

Troodon moms laid two eggs a day over a week or so, and *Troodon* moms and dads may have protected the nest, unlike most dinosaur parents.

Troodon had unusually large eyes, perfectly made for seeing prey in low light.

Eat all

You might think such a clever beast was a sly predator. In fact, it may have eaten fruit and nuts and little animals, whatever it could find in a tough, cold world.

Reptile civilization

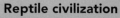

In 1982 Canadian paleontologist Dale Russell wondered what might have happened if *Troodon* had survived the great dinosaur extinction. Maybe with its super brain, binocular vision, and upright walk, it could have become the clever ruler of the planet, like humans are today. But *Troodon* was probably no smarter than a chicken!

VS STRUTHIOMIMUS

Few ancient dinosaurs looked more like modern ostriches and emus than *Struthiomimus*. No wonder its name means "ostrich mimic." It even had a birdlike beak. And with two strong, ostrichlike hind legs and three-toed feet, it could probably run very fast, like ostriches do.

Long, pointy birdlike beak with no teeth.

Struthiomimus *had a very long, very bendy neck, suggesting it got most of its food from the ground.*

Struthiomimus *may have had stripes along its body for camouflage.*

Mixed diet

Experts debate over just what *Struthiomimus* ate. It belongs to a family of birdlike dinosaurs a bit like theropods, such as *T. rex*, which was an out-and-out carnivore. But most experts think *Struthiomimus* ate a little bit of everything, from plants one day to worms and little creatures the next.

NAME: Ostrich mimic
TIME: 83–66 mya
HABITAT: Plains
DIET: Omnivore
LOCATION: North America

Just how fast?

Nobody really knows how fast *Struthiomimus* could run. It certainly had long, strong ostrichlike legs, great for high speed. But it was also pretty heavy, weighing about 330 pounds. So its top speed could have been anything from thirty to fifty mph or more.

VELOCIRAPTOR VS

Very fast and nimble, *Velociraptors* were tiny for dinosaurs but made up for it in ferocity! Hunting mostly alone, they relied on ambush rather than chasing down prey. After pouncing, they'd jab their savage claws to grip their victim, while tearing at the flesh with their teeth.

The feathered arms may have been for show or for covering eggs in the nest.

Velociraptors had feathers and small wings, but couldn't fly.

Killing claw?
A V*elociraptor* held the deadly claw on its second toe high to keep it supersharp. Scientists once thought it lunged with this claw to stab victims. Now they think the claw just gave a formidable grip.

NAME: Swift plunderer
TIME: 75-71 mya
HABITAT: Scrublands and desert
DIET: Lizards, mammals, small dinosaurs
LOCATION: Mongolia

Locked in combat
Seventy million years ago, a *Velociraptor* and *Protoceratops* were locked in deadly combat when they were suddenly overwhelmed by sand—preserving their fight forever in a now-famous fossil discovered in 1971. But *Velociraptor* usually went for smaller prey. So no one knows what provoked this battle.

PROTOCERATOPS

Protoceratops was a small plant-eater, about the size of a pig—except with a truly huge, bony head. It may have roamed the Mongolian desert in vast herds, and more fossils have been found of it than of any other dinosaur. In 2011, a complete nest with fifteen babies was found!

Big head
Protoceratops's skull was huge, with a bony frill around the neck. *Triceratops* perhaps developed its famous horns from *Protoceratops*'s two bony lumps.

Strong teeth and a parrotlike beak were made for gnawing and pulling up tough desert plants. But they could also put up a tough defense!

In the Fighting Dinosaur fossil, Protoceratops has the right forearm of Velociraptor trapped in its beak!

- **NAME:** Early horned face
- **TIME:** 83–72 mya
- **HABITAT:** Scrubland and desert
- **DIET:** Plants
- **LOCATION:** Mongolia

The lion and the eagle
The mythical beast called the griffin has the body of a lion and the head of an eagle. The myth was started by writers in ancient Greece. Some now believe they were simply telling the stories of nomads who found *Protoceratops* fossils in the Gobi Desert.

GIGANOTOSAURUS

Giganotosaurus was an absolute beast! One of the biggest land predators ever after *Spinosaurus*, *Giganotosaurus* was not quite so heavy and strong as *T. rex*, but taller and much faster. It's probable that packs of *Giganotosaurus* brought down *Argentinosaurus*, perhaps the largest land animal ever.

The small size of its braincase shows it wasn't quite as brainy as T. rex.

Giganotosaurus *was not only fast, it was probably agile, too, able to make fast turns because its long, thin tail kept its balance.*

Slasher
Giganotosaurus had a huge skull with sharp teeth. But its jaws weren't quite so big and much less powerful then *T. rex*'s, so it probably inflicted slicing wounds rather than bites. That would have helped it bring down prey too big to wrap its claws around.

Giganotosaurus *had short arms and three-fingered, clawed hands.*

- **NAME:** Giant southern lizard
- **TIME:** Around 96 mya
- **HABITAT:** Forests and plains
- **DIET:** Large dinosaurs
- **LOCATION:** Argentina

Remains to be seen
The first *Giganotosaurus* remains were found in Argentina only in 1993. No complete skeleton has yet been found. Nor have remains of juveniles. So there's still a lot to learn about it. By the way, *Giganotosaurus* should not be confused with *Gigantosaurus*, a smaller herbivore from Britain.

VS PARASAUROLOPHUS

You can always recognize a *Parasaurolophus* by its amazing, long, hollow bony crest. Experts once thought the crest might be a snorkel for foraging underwater. But now they suspect it was a kind of trumpet for making a loud, booming noise. It helped the animals herd together in dense forests, and sounded the alarm.

What's the duckbill?

Parasaurolophus was a kind of hadrosaur, a family of dinosaurs known as the duckbills. Hadrosaurs had a wide beak, yes, but they didn't look that much like ducks and their jaws were full of teeth.

Parasaurolophus mostly walked on four legs. But it could also rear up to reach food in the trees and possibly run.

The crest was up to six feet long.

NAME: Next to Saurolophus
TIME: 76.5–73 mya
HABITAT: Dense forests
DIET: Pine needles and other leaves
LOCATION: North America

HONK

Parasaurolophus skull

High and low

Experts think that the noise the crest made changed as *Parasaurolophus* grew. From looking at crests and ear cavities, they think that juveniles could hear and make high-pitched sounds. Adults, however, had less sharp hearing but could make a louder, deeper boom, a change a bit like in human voices!

Dino news

Two centuries ago, no one knew dinosaurs existed. But since then, we have found out an incredible amount about them, and more is being discovered all the time. Even if you're a big dino fan, here are ten things even you may not know.

Nodosaurus *was an eighteen-foot herbivore from Late Cretaceous times. It was covered in spikes with a tail that could shred an enemy.*

1. *Archaeopteryx* was the first, early birdlike dinosaur found. A fossil, 150 million years old, has the imprint of feathered bird wings and a long dinosaur tail. Now experts are convinced *Archaeopteryx* could fly in a way unlike any bird today, and had black or black-tipped wings.

2. *Suzhousaurus* is a recently found dinosaur that stands on two legs. It looks like an overfed rat with a small head, or a giant sloth. It's related to *T. rex* but was an herbivore.

3. Sleeping giant
One of the best-preserved dinosaur fossils ever found was that of a *Nodosaurus* in Canada in 2011. It was not just the skeleton, but the whole body, scales and all. It looked like it was asleep.

4. Old dinos Big carnivores like *T. rex* lived for about thirty years, but big herbivores may have lived for much longer. Some could have lived for eighty years.

Sixty-foot Alamosaurus *probably lived as long as an elephant—about eighty years.*

5. *Camarasaurus* Recent finds suggest that family groups of the large sauropod *Camarasaurus* could have migrated long distances to find food as the seasons changed, maybe making an 1,800-mile round trip each year.

6. *Pegomastax* was first properly described in 2012. Pretty weird, you could say it was a cross between a porcupine and parrot, with a back covered in sharp spines and a beak with teeth that sharpened themselves against one another.

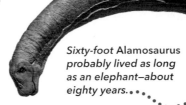

Camarasaurus, a sixty-foot giant, lived during Jurassic times.

7. Dragon's teeth China is rich in fossils. The ancient Chinese discovered prehistoric teeth. Some believed they were dragon teeth, though they were in fact from early mammals. Studying fossil teeth gives scientists essential information, proving, for example, that *T. rex* never chewed. It bit chunks out of prey and swallowed them whole!

8. Hellboy In 2015, fossil hunters discovered a new species of horned dinosaur called *Regaliceratops*. It had such a fantastic crowned frill that they nicknamed it Hellboy, after the cartoon character.

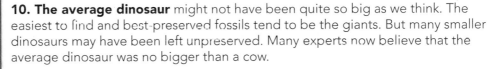

9. Heaviest *T. rex*
In 2019, the world met a heavyweight champ *T. rex*, Scotty. Its fossil skeleton was estimated to be even more massive than the previous champ, Sue. Scotty weighed 19,555 pounds, as much as 6.5 Volkswagen Beetles.

T. rex probably had about 300 bones.

10. The average dinosaur might not have been quite so big as we think. The easiest to find and best-preserved fossils tend to be the giants. But many smaller dinosaurs may have been left unpreserved. Many experts now believe that the average dinosaur was no bigger than a cow.

MAPUSAURUS VS

No one thought predators could ever bring down a mighty *Argentinosaurus*, one of the largest creatures that ever lived on land. But then they found *Mapusaurus* fossils in groups. So experts wondered if *Mapusaurus* hunted in packs. Working together, such ferocious gangs might have attacked even the biggest giants.

Monster killer
At forty feet long or more, *Mapusaurus* was one of the biggest predators ever, only truly outsized by *Spinosaurus*.

The skulls were huge but fairly light because of hollows in the bone structure.

- **NAME:** Earth lizard
- **TIME:** 99–90 mya
- **HABITAT:** Scrub and semi-desert
- **DIET:** Medium and large dinosaurs
- **LOCATION:** Argentina

Mapusaurus had a giant jaw full of knife-sharp slicing teeth, perfect for ripping a chunk out of Argentinosaurus, *then speeding off.*

Stamped
Even in packs, *Mapusaurus* had to be superwary when attacking a giant *Argentinosaurus*. One mistake, and splat! Crunch time! *Mapusaurus* were big, but *Argentinosaurus* were twice as big!

Jumble of bones
Mapusaurus was only discovered in 1995, when experts discovered a jumble of bones in South America. It took years for them to figure out just what they'd found—a giant, forty-foot predator, along with seven of its kind of various different ages.

ARGENTINOSAURUS

It's almost impossible to imagine how big *Argentinosaurus* was. It was absolutely colossal! It was as heavy as an entire herd of African elephants and three times as tall as a giraffe. It could only lumber along at five mph, but with that size, you don't need to run from anything!

Stretchy neck
Argentinosaurus had a long, bendy neck for stripping leaves from trees. But no one knows how it lifted it. It may have eaten a ton of food a day, and pooped half a ton!

Argentinosaurus had shin bones as thick as a tree trunk and almost as tall as a human.

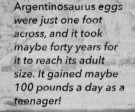

Argentinosaurus eggs were just one foot across, and it took maybe forty years for it to reach its adult size. It gained maybe 100 pounds a day as a teenager!

NAME: Argentine lizard
TIME: 94–90 mya
HABITAT: Forest and scrub
DIET: Plants
LOCATION: Argentina

Guesswork
Most of what we know about *Argentinosaurus* is speculation. All that's been found of it so far is a few ribs, a few spine bones, and two mighty leg bones. But we can work out its likely size by comparing these with other, smaller sauropod bones. It's exciting work!

Dinobusters

Dinosaurs developed attack and defense capabilities to become all-time champs. Here's a rundown of the gold medalists in the prehistoric Olympics, some of the most extreme animals to have ever lived.

THE LONGEST HORN The record for the longest horn goes to . . . *Triceratops*. A *Triceratops*'s two brow horns were maybe four feet long. One youngster known as Yoshi's Trike was found with horns almost 3.8 feet long—so they could have grown much longer.

THE FASTEST Many of the strongest entrants for best dinosaur sprinter were ostrich-like dinosaurs such as *Dromiceiomimus*, which could reach thirty mph. But the gold medalist may have been the tiny *Compsognathus*, which could occasionally reach fifty mph.

THE LONGEST NECK *Sauroposeidon* really stuck its neck out. It was once thought that *Sauroposeidon*'s neck was fifty-five feet long. That's been downgraded to thirty-nine feet, but still head and shoulders above the competition.

FASTEST ON FOUR The fastest dinosaurs were all two-legged. That's unlike today, where four-legged mammals like the cheetah can be superfast. The fastest four-legged dino was *Parasaurolophus*, which could just about make twenty-five mph.

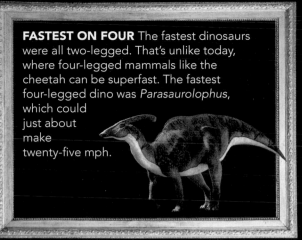

THE LONGEST TAIL When it comes to tails, no one can beat *Diplodocus*. *Diplodocus* had the longest tail of any creature that ever lived, over forty-five feet. No one knows why.

THE STRONGEST The giant herbivores had to be pretty strong to move all that weight But the strongest predator was probably *T. rex*. Its bite alone had a force of 8,000 lbs.

8,000 LBS

THE DUMBEST The dunce of the dino world was *Stegosaurus*. It was bigger than an elephant yet had a brain the size of a Brazil nut. But that was all it needed for its simple life.

THE BIGGEST No complete dino skeleton has ever been found, so the jury is still out. But the heavyweight champ is probably *Argentinosaurus*—maybe 100 feet or more long and as heavy as a herd of African elephants at between sixty and ninety tons.

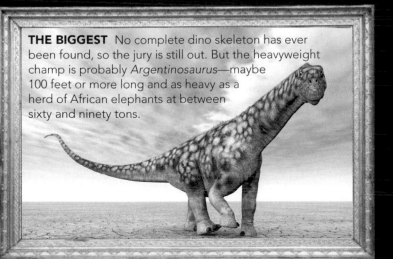

THE BRAINIEST The mastermind of the dino world was *Troodon*. This smallish predator, with stereoscopic vision and proper hands, at least had the biggest brain for its size of any dino. Still, that was no bigger than a chicken's brain.

DEINONYCHUS

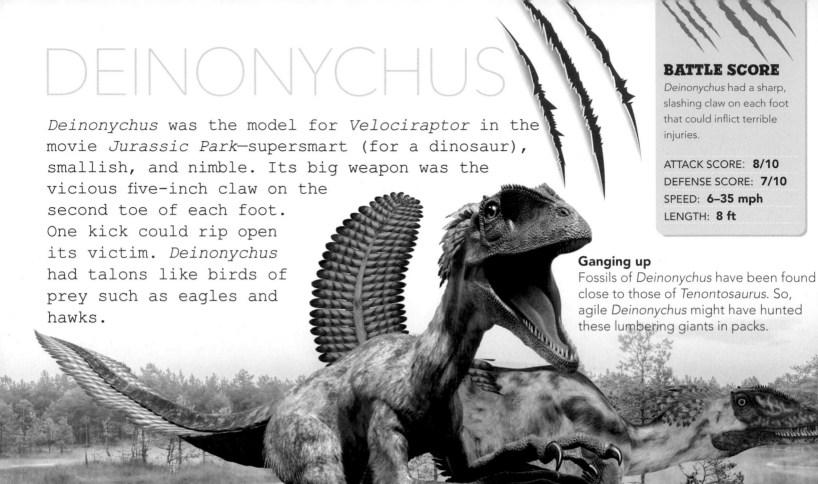

Deinonychus was the model for *Velociraptor* in the movie *Jurassic Park*—supersmart (for a dinosaur), smallish, and nimble. Its big weapon was the vicious five-inch claw on the second toe of each foot. One kick could rip open its victim. *Deinonychus* had talons like birds of prey such as eagles and hawks.

BATTLE SCORE
Deinonychus had a sharp, slashing claw on each foot that could inflict terrible injuries.

ATTACK SCORE: **8/10**
DEFENSE SCORE: **7/10**
SPEED: **6–35 mph**
LENGTH: **8 ft**

Ganging up
Fossils of *Deinonychus* have been found close to those of *Tenontosaurus*. So, agile *Deinonychus* might have hunted these lumbering giants in packs.

How fast?
Experts differ widely on how fast *Deinonychus* was. Some say it was speedier than a racehorse. Others say it was barely faster than human walking pace. You decide!

Long fingers with claws for gripping and grasping.

- **NAME:** Terrible claw
- **TIME:** 125–100 mya
- **HABITAT:** Swamps
- **DiET:** Small and medium dinosaurs
- **LOCATION:** North America

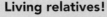

Living relatives!
It was *Deinonychus* fossils that persuaded some experts that birds are descended from dinosaurs. This idea is now widely accepted. *Deinonychus* had a rather birdlike shape and may even have had some feathers.

VS SAUROPELTA

Spiky! *Sauropelta* might have been a shuffling plant-eater, but even the most vicious predator would have thought twice about tackling this tank of a dinosaur. Its body was not only supertough but covered in enough spines and studs to break your teeth wherever you tried to bite!

Beaky

Sauropelta was not quite toothless. But it relied on its wide beak for tearing the needles off pine trees and ferns. *Sauropelta* was as heavy as the biggest rhino, the extinct northern white rhino, at over 1.6 tons.

The spines on Sauropelta's neck were seriously impressive. Some experts think they were mainly for show rather than for defense.

Sauropelta's tail was half the length of its body and covered in bony nodules.

NAME: Lizard shield
TIME: 125–100 mya
HABITAT: Forested floodplains
DIET: Plants
LOCATION: North America

Guesswork

T. rex, with its bone-crushing jaw, might have got to grips with *Sauropelta*, but *T. rex* only appeared tens of millions of years after *Sauropelta's* time. So adult *Sauropelta* probably lived a sedate, untroubled life.

ZZZZZ

SPINOSAURUS **VS**

Spinosaurus was simply the biggest predator that ever lived on land, bigger even than *T. rex* and *Giganotosaurus*. But it was not that scary if you could run fast. It was in water that it was really deadly. It preyed mainly on big river fish such as giant coelacanths and sawfish, which it snapped up with ease.

Sail back
Spinosaurus gets its name from the big sail on its back, made from spines up to five feet long, webbed with skin. No one knows what it was for. It may have helped control body temperature.

Recent research suggests *Spinosaurus had a paddle-like tail for driving it fast through the water.*

NAME: Spine lizard
TIME: 112–97 mya
HABITAT: Swamps
DIET: Big fish
LOCATION: North Africa

Spinosaurus had the longest head of any meat-eating dinosaur, six feet long. It was like a crocodile's head, with teeth that were straight points.

Flying dinner
Although it was fish who really had to watch out for *Spinosaurus*, the remains of a pterosaur—a giant flying reptile—were found with a *Spinosaurus* tooth embedded. So although it was pretty slow-moving on land, those jaws could be fatal for the unwary.

Fossil *Spinosaurus* tooth

OURANOSAURUS

Ouranosaurus was an early hadrosaur relative, a duck-billed dinosaur. Unlike other hadrosaurs, it had no crest. Instead, it seems likely it had a big, bony sail on its back—just like the monster *Spinosaurus*, which also lived near the same swamps and rivers, and may have preyed on it.

- **NAME:** Brave lizard
- **TIME:** 115–100 mya
- **HABITAT:** River delta
- **DIET:** Plants
- **LOCATION:** Africa

Summer sail
Ouranosaurus's sail back was two or three feet high. No one knows what it was for, but experts guess it might have been a solar panel for soaking up heat and cooling.

The flat skull was two feet long and filled with hundreds of teeth, tailor-made for chewing tough plants like cycads.

The tail was heavy, maybe to give balance when Ouranosaurus *stood up* on its back legs to reach leaves high up.

Ouranosaurus could stand up and run on two legs, but its feet were too narrow and its tail too short to balance well when running.

Saharan wanderer
Remains of *Ouranosaurus* were found in the 1960s in the Sahara desert in modern-day Niger. One hundred million years ago, of course, the area was wet and forested. It was given its name by a French team of experts from an Arabic word for "courage."

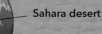

Sahara desert

UTAHRAPTOR

Utahraptor was a killing machine, maybe one of the biggest raptors that ever lived, the king-size version of the later *Deinonychus* and *Velociraptor*. Like modern birds of prey, raptor dinosaurs, or *Dromaeosaurus*, had deadly claws. And *Utahraptor* had the biggest of all, nine inches of flesh-ripping power on the second toe of each foot.

The smaller raptor dinosaurs seemed to hunt in packs, and there's every chance that Utahraptors did, too. Terrifying!

Slasher
Utahraptor didn't kill its victims instantly. It could have used a grip-and-rip method, digging into the victim's flesh until it was exhausted, or slicing deadly wounds so that it bled to death.

- **NAME:** Utah plunderer
- **TIME:** 130–122 mya
- **HABITAT:** Floodplains and riverside forest
- **DIET:** Large dinosaurs such as *Iguanodons*
- **LOCATION:** North America

Birds of a feather
Although they couldn't fly, raptor dinosaurs are highly likely to have had feathers, just like today's raptor birds—and so, probably, did *Utahraptor*. It may even have had warm blood.

Dino star
Utahraptor is a superstar. It starred in its own film, *Raptor Red*, an adventure about a female *Utahraptor* and her young. And it is Utah's state dinosaur, pushing aside *Allosaurus*, which is now the state fossil.

PRODUCTION
DIRECTOR
SCENE   TAKE   ROLL
DATE

VS MICRORAPTOR

Microraptor was one of the first climbing, flying, non-bird dinosaurs to be discovered. It had four feathered wings and a feathered tail! It hunted lizards in the treetops and caught giant dragonflies in midair.

Microraptor would jump from tree to tree, gliding on its four wings. Some experts believe it could fly by flapping its wings.

Takeoff

When *Microraptor* was discovered in China in 2000, scientists were stunned. Its feathers were obvious. And they weren't just fluffy for keeping warm. They were long flight feathers!

Microraptor might have been awkward on the ground, its feathered limbs making it very ungainly.

NAME: Small plunderer
TIME: 125–120 mya
HABITAT: Forested floodplains
DIET: Small lizards and insects
LOCATION: China

Those claws look vicious, but the chances are they weren't for grasping prey but for gripping onto bark to make a quick getaway from predators.

Lizard for lunch

In 2019, scientists found a new species of lizard. They found it in the stomach of a *Microraptor*! It was whole and probably eaten headfirst. This was the first fossil to show that the dinosaur ate lizards.

SINOSAUROPTERYX

Sinosauropteryx was the first dinosaur fossil ever found with feathers, and the first dinosaur we know the color of: reddish-orange. The discovery of this little predator in China in 1994 was clear evidence that dinosaurs are related to modern birds. Yet *Sinosauropteryx* was an early relative of *T. rex*—small but very fierce.

Sinosauropteryx had a dark eye mask like a pirate!

Counter-cover
Sinosauropteryx were dark on top and light underneath. This kind of camouflage is called counter-shading. It reverses the normal pattern of shade created by the sun in the daytime, confusing the eye and making it harder to spot.

Coat of feathers
Sinosauropteryx's feathers may have helped keep it warm, suggesting it might have been warm-blooded. But they may also have provided camouflage, or just been for show. The feathers weren't like modern bird feathers, but a fur-like mat called pelage.

The long tail had distinctive bands of orange and white.

- **NAME:** Chinese lizard wing
- **TIME:** 135–120 mya
- **HABITAT:** Open plains
- **DIET:** Small reptiles and mammals
- **LOCATION:** China

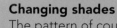

Changing shades
The pattern of counter-shading suggested to experts that *Sinosauropteryx* lived in open grassland. Animals living in open grassland often have a change from dark to light high up on their bodies and quite suddenly. This pattern works well to camouflage them in direct sunlight.

VS IGUANODON

Iguanodon was one of the first dinosaurs to be named, in 1825. No one knew about dinosaurs then, and that the world was once ruled by giant reptiles. English geologist Gideon Mantell and his wife, Mary Ann, found what looked like the tooth of an iguana—only bigger. So the dinosaur is called *Iguanodon*, or iguana tooth.

It had sharp teeth, such as the one the Mantells found, great for chewing but not biting.

Not an iguana at all!
Later discoveries showed *Iguanodon* is not like an iguana at all. It was a big ornithopod (bird-foot) dinosaur that spent most of its time on all fours. *Iguanodon* browsed on horsetail ferns, cycads, and conifers. It had a sharp beak for yanking them off, then snipping them like shears.

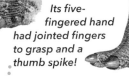

Its five-fingered hand had jointed fingers to grasp and a thumb spike!

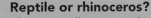

- **NAME:** Iguana tooth
- **TIME:** 130–125 mya
- **HABITAT:** Varied
- **DIET:** Plants
- **LOCATION:** Americas and Eurasia

Reptile or rhinoceros?
The Mantells were only amateur fossil collectors. Gideon was convinced that the giant tooth that had come into his possession was from a plant-eating giant from the Mesozoic age. But when he showed it to the professionals, they doubted him. It was only after a lot of persistence that he persuaded them at last that giant reptiles once lived on Earth.

Dino parents

For a long time, experts assumed that dinosaurs hatched from hard eggs, because that's all that was ever found as fossils. Now fossils of soft eggs have been found, like those of turtles and other reptiles today. It's also become clear that every kind of dinosaur parent was different. Most left their eggs and chicks to make their own way in the world, but some took care of their young.

Maiasaura model

Soft eggs were buried, but hard eggs were laid in hollows. *Maiasaura* nested in colonies, packed with nests dug out of the dirt. Rotting plants were placed on the eggs to keep them warm.

This is a model of a Maiasaura nest with eggs and hatchlings.

Babysitter

Some dinosaur moms brooded, sitting on their eggs like modern birds do. When the first oviraptorid dinosaur fossil was found, it had two eggs with it. Experts thought they were stolen. Then in 1994, a fossil of *Citipati* was found in Mongolia, sitting on a big nest of eggs, clearly its own.

Oviraptor

Growing up

When *Maiasaura* were born, their legs weren't fully developed. But fossil baby *Maiasaura* teeth are worn. So it seems likely that their parents protected them and brought food to the nest. It's possible that parental care continued until the juveniles could keep up with the herd. Like modern sea turtles, *Maiasaura* returned to lay their eggs in the place where they were born.

Even with a caring parent, it's likely that 90 percent of Maiasaura didn't survive their first year.

Young dinosaurs may have stayed with their siblings while growing up for protection.

Blue eggs

Not all dinosaur eggs were white. Experts have found recently that they can figure out what colors they might have been. Just like birds' eggs today, the colors were unique to the species. *Deinonychus* eggs were probably a blue-green color.

Compsognathus may have been small—no bigger than a turkey—but it was fierce and very, very fast.
It may be one of the fastest two-legged creatures ever, easily outrunning an ostrich, and it had large eyes to catch speedy prey such as small lizards.

COMPSOGNATHUS

It had a long tail to keep it balanced on high-speed turns.

Snatch to the hatch
Compsognathus's main weapons were its pincerlike front claws. It had two on each hand and would use them to snatch prey and cram it into its long mouth.

It may have had a downy coat of short feathers.

- **NAME:** Elegant jaw
- **TIME:** 155–145 mya
- **HABITAT:** Lagoons
- **DIET:** Small reptiles and mammals
- **LOCATION:** Western Europe

Lizards for lunch
Only two *Compsognathus* skeletons have been found, but both have had complete lizards in their stomachs. That shows how quick this dinosaur was, because lizards are not easy to catch. It also shows they were swallowed whole, without chewing!

VS SEISMOSAURUS

When *Seismosaurus* was first discovered in New Mexico, it was called earthshaker, or *Seismosaurus*, because it seemed so gigantic it must have made the earth shake as it moved. Experts estimated it was 150-170 feet long, longer than any other dinosaur. It's been downgraded considerably. It may be just a big *Diplodocus*, but it's still a giant.

Like all Diplodocus, Seismosaurus *had a long tail, helping to balance its long neck.*

Neck and neck
Seismosaurus had one of the longest necks of any land animal ever—up to forty feet. So it wouldn't have needed to move its feet much—one giant sweep of its neck could cover a lot of plants!

The whipping tail would have broken the sound barrier and created a loud sonic boom.

- **NAME:** Earth-shaking lizard
- **TIME:** 159-144 mya
- **HABITAT:** Forests
- **DIET:** Plants
- **LOCATION:** Southern North America

Seismosaurus *probably weighed as little as twenty-five tons, way down from original estimates, but still pretty hefty.*

Heads up
Experts have wondered how *Seismosaurus*'s heart could have pumped blood all the way up its neck. Some experts suggest this means it could never have been warm-blooded. Some also believe that the animal never lifted its head and simply swept the ground like a giant vacuum cleaner.

ALLOSAURUS VS

Allosaurus was one of the first giant super killers. About the same size as *T. rex*, it was a match for pretty much any animal alive at the time. It was much weaker than *T. rex* but much, much faster, and with a bit of binocular vision, it could home in on prey from a distance with deadly accuracy.

Allosaurus, unusually, had a pair of small horns above its eyes.

The skull was narrow but strong.

The seventy teeth curved backward, better for slashing and pulling its victim's flesh down its throat.

Allosaurus had strong hind limbs, and each foot had three weight-bearing toes.

- **NAME:** Different lizard
- **TIME:** 156–150 mya
- **HABITAT:** Semi-arid plains
- **DIET:** Large dinosaurs
- **LOCATION:** North America

It had big, nasty claws, which it may have used to pin its prey to stop it escaping.

Open wide
Allosaurus's fearsome jaw could gape amazingly wide, wider than a crocodile's. This may have helped it use its vicious teeth to slash down through its victim's flesh like a multiblade knife.

T. rex

Not so different
Allosaurus was called the "different" lizard because its backbone was unlike that of any other dinosaur's when it was first discovered. Now many more *Allosaurus* fossils have been found, especially in Utah, Wyoming, and Colorado, and it is one of the best-known predatory dinosaurs.

STEGOSAURUS

Stegosaurus was about the size of a rhino but equipped with a row of armored plates and tail spikes that made it a tough nut to crack. *Allosaurus* was a big beast with mighty weaponry, and fossils show *Stegosaurus* often lived to tell the tale after a fight—with broken spines and *Allosaurus* teeth embedded.

Stegosaurus was not a mastermind. It had a brain smaller than a dog's. But then, it had a pretty simple lifestyle, munching plants.

The back plates may have helped regulate temperature.

Experts found an *Allosaurus* with a wound from a *Stegosaurus* tail that was likely fatal!

Stegosaurus ambled along at human walking pace, walking on its toes.

Back plate
Stegosaurus had a spectacular roof of dorsal plates along its back that provided its main defense against *Allosaurus*, but may also have been for show. They may have been covered in colorful keratin—the material of human fingernails and birds' beaks.

- **NAME:** Roof lizard
- **TIME:** 150 mya
- **HABITAT:** Forests and bushy plains
- **DIET:** Plants
- **LOCATION:** Europe and eastern North America

Tail end
A *Stegosaurus*'s tail was studded with four spikes called thagomizers. The name came from a funny cartoon, and it stuck! Some experts believe that *Stegosaurus* used thagomizers to slash wounds in predators such as *Allosaurus*, and drove them so far into an attacker's skeleton that they broke!

CERATOSAURUS **VS**

Ceratosaurus was a serious predator with a killer streak. It was a little smaller, slower, and less strong than its contemporary, *Allosaurus*. In a standoff, over a corpse, *Allosaurus* would win any day. They both lived in the same areas. But maybe *Ceratosaurus* stayed near the swamps and hunted water creatures to avoid competing directly.

Ceratosaurus had two short brow ridges, and bony knobs and ridges above its eyes and on the top of its head.

Notable nose
What made *Ceratosaurus* stand out was the short horn on the end of its nose. It was probably just for display.

The deep, long, crocodilian tail was well adapted for swimming.

When in the water, Ceratosaurus preyed on big lungfish, crocodiles, and turtles.

NAME: Horned lizard
TIME: 161–145 mya
HABITAT: Swamps
DIET: Meat, fish, and reptiles
LOCATION: Southern North America and Africa

Teaming up
Ceratosaurus may have hunted in packs. They were quite brainy for early dinosaurs, and they might occasionally have competed with *Allosaurus* for the same prey, including *Iguanodon*, *Stegosaurus*, and even large sauropods. But when it came to a standoff, they'd probably back down.

APATOSAURUS

Apatosaurus was one of the biggest animals that ever lived, a walking, towering mountain. It was vulnerable to predators when young, but once it was fully grown it was usually too much for even the biggest predators to take on, especially since its vulnerable neck and head were so high.

BATTLE SCORE

Apatosaurus was a true heavyweight bruiser, weighing more than three school buses put together

ATTACK SCORE: **3/10**
DEFENSE SCORE: **8/10**
SPEED: **12 mph**
LENGTH: **70–90 ft**

Heavy meal
Amazingly, *Apatosaurus* had few teeth. It swallowed vegetation whole and then swallowed stones to help break food down in its stomach!

No one knows just how this giant creature managed to lay eggs—but it did!

The long neck mowed wide swathes of vegetation, reaching mosses and ferns in swampy areas not safe for heavyweights!

NAME: Deceptive lizard
TIME: 161–145 mya
HABITAT: Forests and busy plains
DIET: Plants
LOCATION: North America

Bone wars
When dinosaur hunter Othniel C. Marsh found a fossil *Apatosaurus* in 1879, it was so big he thought it must be a new species. He called it a *Brontosaurus*. In 1903, Elmer Riggs showed it was just a big *Apatosaurus* . But *Brontosaurus* was already a superstar. Now *Apatosaurus* and *Brontosaurus* are recognized once more as different kinds of dinosaurs.

MONOLOPHOSAURUS

Monolophosaurus was half the size of *T. rex*, but it was one of the rulers of its time, and is a little like the mighty *Allosaurus* from later times. Except *Monolophosaurus* had a weird, knobbly crest on its snout. This crest is what gives it its name and is unique.

Gotcha!
Monolophosaurus probably used speed and surprise to catch its prey. Even fellow killers like *Dilophosaurus* may have been ambushed and vanquished by a top *Monolophosaurus*.

Boom box
No one knows what the crest was for, but it contains hollows. These hollows may have reverberated like a drum to give *Monolophosaurus* an absolutely terrifying roar.

Monolophosaurus had long, strong hind limbs, giving a good turn of speed in the chase.

- **NAME:** Single-crested lizard
- **TIME:** 167–161 mya
- **HABITAT:** Forests
- **DIET:** Other dinosaurs
- **LOCATION:** China

The teeth were supersharp, backward-curving blades that sliced deep into flesh.

Mystery dinosaur
Only one not-entirely-complete fossil of *Monolophosaurus* has been found. So experts are not sure quite how it fits into the picture. Some say it's related to another, smaller Chinese crested predator, *Guanlong*, which could have been an ancestor of *T. rex*. Others say it's not.

T. rex   *Monolophosaurus*

VS KENTROSAURUS

They may have been placid plant-eaters, but all stegosaurs had spectacular spikes and plates to protect them. And of all the stegosaurs, *Kentrosaurus* was the most heavily armed, with a double row of back plates right up to its head and an awesome array of spikes.

Like all stegosaurs, Kentrosaurus *had a small head and brain, but quite enough for its simple life.*

Weaponry
Although made of bone, the spikes and plates were not part of *Kentrosaurus*'s skeleton. Instead they were embedded in the skin, like a suit of armor.

That spiky, lashing tail could whip through the air to inflict deadly wounds on any foolhardy assailant.

- **NAME:** Spiky lizard
- **TIME:** 155–151 mya
- **HABITAT:** Forests and bushy plains
- **DIET:** Plants
- **LOCATION:** Africa

Kentrosaurus *was a slow mover, ambling along on four legs. Hunkering down and relying on its armory of spikes was its best defense.*

Jigsaw puzzle
Because the spikes and plates weren't attached directly to the skeleton, no one can be completely sure how they were arranged. They were found loose. So experts have used a lot of guesswork. They can't even be sure the plates were for defense. They may have been for temperature regulation. No one is sure!

Rival monsters

There's no doubt dinosaurs ruled the earth while they were around, but they weren't the only monsters that roamed the planet at the time. It wasn't only dinosaurs like *T. rex* that a hadrosaur might have to watch out for when drinking at the water's edge. All of a sudden, the jaws of *Deinosuchus*, an ancient kind of crocodile, might go SNAP!

Deinosuchus was the top predator of its ecosystem, preying on turtles and dinosaurs its own size!

Deadly *Deinosuchus*
This 29-foot beast prowled the shallow waters of North and Central America. Some experts think it trapped its prey in its jaws then dragged it into the water to drown it, like modern crocodiles.

Teeming with life

Just like today, there were animals at home in every habitat alongside the dinosaurs. There were mammals, though they were mostly small. One badger-sized mammal, *Repenomamus*, was found with the bones of a baby dinosaur in its stomach!

Repenomamus was three feet long, bigger than some of the feathered dinosaurs.

Pterosaurs could dine on dinosaurs the size of a baby horse.

Air combat

We think of birds as the rulers of the air. But in dinosaur times, there was a huge variety of giant, flying reptiles called pterosaurs. Just think of a creature the size of an airplane with a throat as big as a croc swooping down on you.

Some pterosaurs had wingspans as wide as a fighter jet's.

Sea battle

Even If you were far out to sea, you weren't safe from monster reptiles like pliosaurs and plesiosaurs. Will the huge shark in this picture fall prey to the even huger plesiosaur, *Albertonectes*, with its unimaginably long neck?

MOSASAURUS  VS

Terrorizing the oceans for millions of years, mighty *Mosasaurus* was a true monster predator! The daggerlike teeth in its awesome, crocodile-like jaw could stab clean through armored skin. It lurked in the dark to lunge at giant turtles as they came up for air. But it could sometimes run prey down through sheer speed.

BATTLE SCORE

Mosasaurus was huge, very fast, and powerful, with massive jaws lined with daggerlike teeth. It also had excellent eyesight.

ATTACK SCORE: **10/10**
DEFENSE SCORE: **10/10**
SPEED: **Unknown**
LENGTH: **50 ft**

Mosasaurus could have been over fifty feet long. That's quite a lot longer than a school bus.

The four flippers provided steering and an extra burst of speed for a lightning lunge.

A second set of teeth right inside the mouth finishes the job of ripping flesh.

- **NAME:** Meuse River lizard
- **TIME:** 71-66 mya
- **HABITAT:** Oceans
- **DIET:** Sharks, giant turtles, and sea lizards
- **LOCATION:** Atlantic Ocean and global

Jaws of death

Like snakes, *Mosasaurus* had a double-hinged jaw and a flexible skull. This allowed the mouth to gape very wide, so *Mosasaurus* could down prey almost whole.

Meuse monster

In 1764, a *Mosasaurus* skull was found near the city of Maastricht in the Netherlands, showing that there were once-giant creatures now extinct. Native Americans had long known of such fossils, too, and thought they were remains of mythological beasts such as Unktehila.

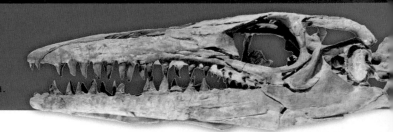

ALBERTONECTES

Talk about neck! *Albertonectes* had the longest neck for its body of any animal ever! Its mega neck was more than twenty-three feet—twice as long as its body. No one knows quite why. Maybe it was for reaching down to vacuum shellfish off the seafloor. But it would have been hard for fish and squid to know which way to swim to escape with that fearsome maw writhing in every direction.

Neck and neck

No other creature has ever had as many cervical vertebrae (neck bones) as *Albertonectes*, 76 in all! Some land dinosaurs, such as *Mamenchisaurus*, had necks almost twice as long, but their necks were more in proportion to their bodies and they only had 19 neck bones or fewer.

Albertonectes swam by sweeping its flippers up and down like wings.

NAME: Alberta swimmer
TIME: 83–71 mya
HABITAT: Oceans
DIET: Fish, squid, and shellfish
LOCATION: Global

Loch Ness monster

Is there a monster in Scotland's deepest lake, Loch Ness? That's what some people say! Blurred photos showing a long neck suggest that "Nessie" is a plesiosaur, a prehistoric marine reptile like *Albertonectes*. But scientific searches have come up with nothing.

LIOPLEURODON VS

If you dare go into the water in Jurassic times, you need to be afraid of *Liopleurodon*—very afraid. This awesome predator was as big as a killer whale, with jaws as deadly as a crocodile's. It was one of the most remarkable predators in the ocean shallows of all time.

Liopleurodon breathed air through nostrils on top of its snout, and every now and then would have to come up to the surface for a breather.

- **NAME:** Smooth-sided teeth
- **TIME:** 165–161 mya
- **HABITAT:** Ocean shallows
- **DIET:** Squid and marine reptiles
- **LOCATION:** Oceans

Four-flipper drive

Liopleurodon might lie waiting, deep down in the shadows. Then it might surge up at speed to catch its unsuspecting prey and rip it to pieces in fearsome jaws. *Liopleurodon* had huge flippers, which it beat up and down to fly through the water, like a turtle. These gave it a big burst of speed in pursuit of its prey.

Scent was the giveaway for prey. **Liopleurodon** *had strong scent detectors and could pick up a trace from some distance.*

Three-tooth

For a long while, *Liopleurodon* was known from just three big teeth. We now know it's a marine reptile called a pliosaur, which ruled the Jurassic oceans with plesiosaurs. Pliosaurs had big heads and stocky bodies. Plesiosaurs had smaller heads and were more streamlined.

STENOPTERYGIUS

Stenopterygius was the dolphin of its time. It was, of course, a reptile, not a mammal. But it was of a similar streamlined shape and a superfast swimmer. It had a much longer, missile-like snout, packed with little, sharp teeth. It may have hunted in family groups.

Stenopterygius had four flippers, not just two like a dolphin has.

The sleek, vertical tail fin was perfect for high speeds, like that of modern swordfish.

So finny
Stenopterygius had narrow flippers to help it rocket through the water in pursuit of prey. It may have had a top speed of forty mph, charging shoals of fish and isolating some to eat!

- **NAME:** Narrow wing
- **TIME:** 183–171 mya
- **HABITAT:** Ocean shallows
- **DIET:** Small fish and squid
- **LOCATION:** Oceans

Its long, narrow jaws, lined with sharp teeth, were perfect for catching writhing, slippery fish.

Live birth
Stenopterygius belonged to a group of Mesozoic marine reptiles called ichthyosaurs. These creatures lived in the ocean all the time and could not lay eggs. Instead, they gave birth to live young, tailfirst, just like baby dolphins. Little ichthyosaurs swam straight up to the surface for their first breath.

QUETZALCOATLUS

Quetzalcoatlus was a flying creature of truly incredible size, one of the biggest flying creatures ever found. Even standing on the ground it was taller than a giraffe. Imagine a giraffe suddenly flapping wings the size of a small airplane and taking off.

Fabulous flier
Quetzalcoatlus was an amazing flier. Like modern gliders, it relied on air currents rather than continuous flapping. But it could fly 10,000 miles non-stop, and swoop and soar gracefully.

The feet may not have been clawed like those of birds of prey and dinosaurs, but padded for walking on the ground.

Quetzalcoatlus's wingspan was the biggest of any flying creature ever, over thirty feet.

- **NAME:** The Aztec serpent god, Quetzalcoatl
- **TIME:** 72-66 mya
- **HABITAT:** Forested plains and skies
- **DIET:** Small dinosaurs and mammals
- **LOCATION:** Americas

Stalk not stork
Quetzalcoatlus may have done most of its hunting on the ground. It walked well, and stalked prey such as small dinosaurs, snapping them up with a lunge of its giant beak.

How did such a monster take off?
Experts have worked out that *Quetzalcoatlus* could take off quickly using its arms. It crouched down with its wings folded, then pushed itself into the air on its hands, like a kind of handspring or a skier's poles. At once, it would spread its wings and sweep them back and down for extra lift, then start flying.

VS PTERANODON

Pteranodon is one of the best known of the pterosaurs, the giant flying reptiles of the dinosaur age. It wasn't quite as big as its cousin *Quetzalcoatlus*, and had a very different lifestyle. It had a toothless bill, like a pelican's, perfect for catching small fish, and may have spent its life soaring over oceans.

Dive and plunder
Pteranodon had good eyesight and would dive into the water to catch fish with its long bill, then soar away into the sky, with a neat launch from the water's surface.

All pterosaurs had furry bodies and were probably warm-blooded.

Pteranodon had wings up to twenty feet across, supported on the ridiculously long and strong fourth finger of their hands.

Pteranodon could float well and may even have had webbed feet, but probably spent a minimal amount of time in the water.

> **NAME:** Winged toothless
> **TIME:** 81–77 mya
> **HABITAT:** Ocean shallows
> **DIET:** Small fish and shellfish
> **LOCATION:** Oceans

Crests
Many *Pteranodon* species had spectacular bony crests. One species, *P. longiceps,* had a unicorn crest as long as its beak. Most experts think only males had really big crests, and that they were mainly for show. Males were probably bigger all around.

PTERODAUSTRO

Pterodaustro was one of the oddest creatures of the dinosaur age. It was a flying pterosaur, but it was no killing machine. Its amazingly long, upcurved beak was filled not with big, jagged teeth but with thousands of bristles, like a scrubbing brush, for sifting small creatures from the waters of lagoons.

Long, strong arms weren't only for flapping the wings. This pterosaur walked on all fours so it could get its beak down easily to water level.

BATTLE SCORE

Pterodaustro was no predator, unless you're a small water creature, in which case—watch out!

ATTACK SCORE: **1/10**
DEFENSE SCORE: **5/10**
SPEED: **30 mph**
LENGTH: **8 ft**

Fabulous flier
Pterodaustro would dip its beak into the water to scoop out a mouthful, and the bristles would filter out small creatures. The small, top teeth would then crush the creatures for the pterosaur to swallow.

Pterodaustro may have been a beautiful pink, like flamingos today, from the shrimp it ate!

- **NAME:** Wing of the south
- **TIME:** 112–100 mya
- **HABITAT:** Lagoons
- **DIET:** Small water creatures
- **LOCATION:** Argentina and Chile

VS PTERODACTYLUS

Pterodactylus was the first flying reptile discovered, back in 1784, but it was another twenty-five years before experts realized it had wings and could fly. For a long time, it was thought to be the only flying reptile, but we now know of over 200 pterosaurs, and there were certainly many, many more.

Male Pterodactylus *probably had a crest on their heads made of hardened fibers, like the cockscomb of a turkey.*

Water bird

Pterodactylus may have lived in the dinosaur age, but it was not a dinosaur. Nor was it a monster size. It was probably little bigger than a duck and behaved much like a modern seagull, flying by the sea. It could fly well, but its strong legs show that it probably spent much of its time on the ground or in shallow water, foraging for prey including fish.

Pterodactylus *gets its name, meaning wing finger, from the long fourth finger on each hand, which supported the wing.*

- **NAME:** Wing finger
- **TIME:** 155–145 mya
- **HABITAT:** Lake shores
- **DIET:** Small fish and other animals
- **LOCATION:** Africa and Europe

Pterodactylus *was well adapted to life near the water, with webbed feet.*

Dino death

All was going
well for the dinosaurs.
They were the most successful animals on
the planet. Then suddenly, about sixty-six
million years ago, they vanished, almost
all of them, along with their reptile
cousins in the sea and in the sky. All that
was left was fossils. So what went wrong?

Extinction

It seems that 75 percent of life on Earth was wiped out at once. There have been a handful of other similar mass extinctions in Earth's history, but this was one of the worst.

Asteroid strike

The leading suspect for the dinosaurs' demise is a giant asteroid that smashed into the Yucatan Peninsula in Mexico. It vaporized instantly with an explosion millions of times bigger than any nuclear bomb.

Iridium layer

The best evidence that the effect of the asteroid strike was global is a layer of sediment around the world, 11.8 inches thick, that dates from the right time. This layer, the KPg layer, is rich in iridium, an element closely linked to meteorites.

Eruption disruption

Another suspect for dino death is a series of cataclysmic volcanic eruptions in India. The debris may have enveloped the world in dust, turned rain to acid, and blocked out the sun. But an asteroid strike probably fits the dates better.

Survivors

No one knows why, but one family of theropod dinos did make it through—the birds. These miraculous survivors, the cousins of feathered dinosaurs, first appeared some ninety million years ago. From this band of dinosaur survivors came all the 10,000 or so species of birds we know today.

Digging for dinos

We know about dinosaurs because, amazingly, remains of them have been preserved as fossils for millions of years. Mostly, their bodies rotted away long ago. But bones, teeth and claws, and even eggs and footprints are sometimes turned to hard minerals and survive in the ground.

Bones

Sometimes hunters do find complete skeletons, usually flattened by millions of years of rock above them. But mostly, they find just scattered fragments. By comparing with other skeletons, experts can tell a great deal from just a tiny piece.

Dino poop

The technical word for this is coprolite. It's hardened dino poop, and it can tell experts a lot about what dinosaurs ate!

Skin

Experts get very excited when they find a rare fossil that preserves feathers and skin and soft tissue.

Fossilized imprint of *Triceratops* skin

Ankylosaurus footprints

Footprints

In some places, the footprints of dinosaurs made long ago in mud are preserved. These amazing survivors can show how they walked or how fast they ran, or even preserve a chase.

Teeth

Teeth are among the most common fossils. They have such distinctive shapes, and experts can often tell the identity of a dinosaur from just its tooth, as well as what it ate and how it gathered food.

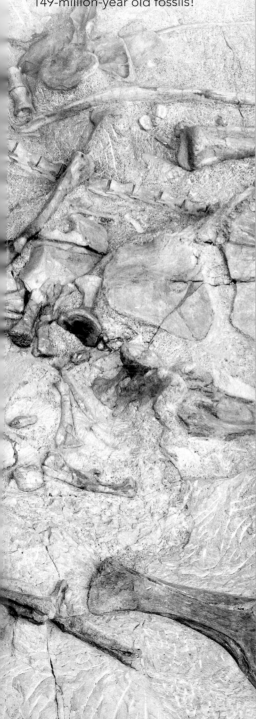

Dinos site
The Quarry Exhibit Hall at the Dinosaur National Monument, USA, is a rock wall with 1,500 bones. There are several places where you can touch these 149-million-year old fossils!

Glossary

Bipedal Walking on two legs.
Carnivore Meat-eater.
Coprolite Fossil of poo.
Cretaceous Geological period that lasted from 145 million to 66 million years ago.
Dromaeosaurs The group of dinosaurs popularly known as raptors.
Hadrosaurs A group of large four-legged herbivorous dinosaurs known as the "duckbills."
Herbivore Plant-eater.
Iguanodons Family of four-legged herbivorous dinosaurs related to hadrosaurs.
Jurassic Geological period that lasted from 200 million to 145 million years.
Keratin A tough protein that makes up hair, skin, and nails.
Meteorite A solid chunk of debris from space that hits the Earth's surface.
Ornithischia "Bird-hipped" herbivorous dinosaurs including stegosaurs, ankylosaurs, cerapods, ornithopods, and pachycephalosaurs.
Pangea The supercontinent that combined all the world's continents in one during the Triassic.
Plesiosaurs Large, long-necked predatory reptiles that lived in the oceans in dinosaur times.
Pliosaurs Large, predatory reptiles with crocodile-like jaws that lived in the oceans in dinosaur times.
Predator Animal that hunts other animals to eat.

Pterosaur Large, long-necked flying reptiles that lived in dinosaur times.
Raptors Small- to medium-sized, birdlike dinosaurs with feathers and a large killing claw on their hind feet.
Saurischia Group of huge dinos with hips like lizards comprised of sauropods and theropods.
Sauropods Means "lizard-footed"—huge four-legged, herbivorous dinosaurs with small heads and long necks and tails.
Stereoscopic or binocular vision Both eyes pointing forward like ours, giving a 3D view of the world, good for judging distance.
Thagomizer Nasty, flailing spikes on a stegosaur's tail.
Theropods Means "beast-footed"—mostly two-legged, short-armed dinosaurs with massive jaws, such as *T. rex* and *Utahraptor*.
Triassic Geological period that lasted from 250 million to 200 million years—and saw the arrival of the dinosaurs.
Tyrannosaurs Terrifying two-legged dino killing machines such as *T. rex* and *Albertosaurus*.

Index

Credits

Written by: John Farndon
Consultant: Carl Mehling, American Museum of Natural History, New York
Art Director: Julia Sabbagh **UK Editor:** Miriam Farbey
US Editor: Ingrid Paredes **US Production Editor:** Jessie Bowman

Photos ©: 7 eyes: OliverChilds/Getty Images; 19 center: Warpaintcobra/Getty Images; 20 left: CoreyFord/Getty Images; 20 center top: Corey Ford/Stocktrek Images/Getty Images; 20 center bottom: CoreyFord/Getty Images; 28 top left: Stocktrek Images/Getty Images; 31 bottom left: MR1805/Getty Images; 31 bottom right: CoreyFord/Getty Images; 35 left: CoreyFord/Getty Images; 35 right: CoreyFord/Getty Images; 38 left: Stocktrek Images, Inc./Alamy Stock Photo; 38 center: Julius T. Csotonyi/Science Source; 41 top: Daniel Eskridge/Dreamstime; 43 center: Nobumichi Tamura/Stocktrek Images/Getty Images; 51 top: mauritius images GmbH/Alamy Stock Photo; 52 bottom: Phil Degginger/Alamy Stock Photo; 62 skin: Corbin17/Alamy Stock Photo; 63 left: Maciej Bledowski/Alamy Stock Photo. All other photos © Shutterstock.com. Illustrations © Scholastic Inc.